2

Sight Words

Written by Shannon Keeley

Illustrations by Ethan Long

An imprint of Sterling Children's Books

This book belongs to

_____

FLASH KIDS, STERLING, and the distinctive Sterling logo are registered trademarks of
Sterling Publishing Co., Inc.

Published by Sterling Publishing Co., Inc.
387 Park Avenue South, New York, NY 10016
Text and illustrations © 2006 by Flash Kids
Distributed in Canada by Sterling Publishing
c/o Canadian Manda Group, 165 Dufferin Street
Toronto, Ontario, Canada M6K 3H6
Distributed in the United Kingdom by GMC Distribution Services
Castle Place, 166 High Street, Lewes, East Sussex, England BN7 1XU
Distributed in Australia by Capricorn Link (Australia) Pty. Ltd.
P.O. Box 704, Windsor, NSW 2756, Australia

Sterling ISBN 978-1-4114-3471-4

Manufactured in China

Lot #:
6 8 10 9 7 5
03/12

For information about custom editions, special sales, premium and
corporate purchases, please contact Sterling Special Sales
Department at 800-805-5489 or specialsales@sterlingpublishing.com.

Cover design and production by Mada Design, Inc.

Dear Parent,

Any time your child reads a text, more than half of the words he or she encounters are sight words. Often, these high-frequency words do not follow regular spelling rules and cannot be "sounded out." So, learning to immediately recognize these words "at sight" is a critical skill for fluent reading. This book covers 24 top sight words and includes lots of practice with tracing and writing, as well as fun word puzzles and games. To get the most from the activities included here, follow these simple steps:

- Find a comfortable place where you and your child can work quietly together.
- Encourage your child to go at his or her own pace.
- Help your child sound out the letters and identify the pictures.
- Offer lots of praise and support.
- Let your child reward his or her work with the included stickers.
- Most of all, remember that learning should be fun! Take time to look at the pictures, laugh at the funny characters, and enjoy this special time spent together.

them

Practice writing the word **them**.

them

Write the word to complete the sentence.

I gave the ball to __ __ __ __ .

Now write your own sentence using the word **them**.

Tic Tac Toe

Circle the row that has the word **them** three times.
Then write **them** three times on the lines below.

them	the	them
thee	them	hem
thm	them	them

like

Practice writing the word **like**.

like like like like like

Write the word to complete the sentence.

I *like* **my pet bird.**

Now write your own sentence using the word **like**.

I like toys!

Word Search

Find the word **like** three times in the word search.

Then write **like** three times on the lines below.

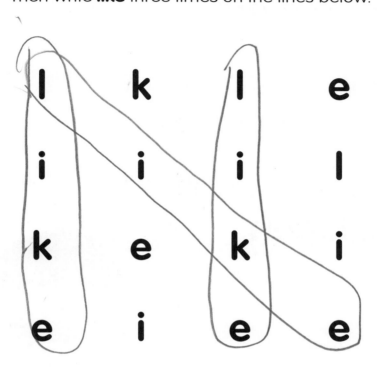

l	k	l	e
i	i	i	l
k	e	k	i
e	i	e	e

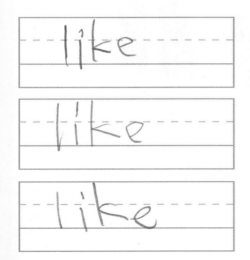

like

like

like

would

Practice writing the word **would**.

would

Write the word to complete the sentence.

I __ __ __ __ __ like to have a kitten.

Now write your own sentence using the word **would**.

Maze

Connect the letters to make **would** and solve the maze!
Then write **would** three times on the lines below.

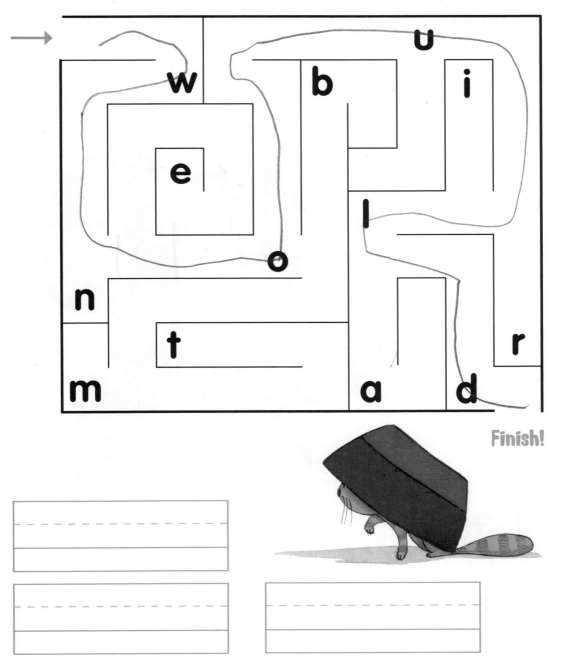

Finish!

come

Practice writing the word **come**.

come

Write the word to complete the sentence.

Please ___ ___ ___ ___ in!

Now write your own sentence using the word **come**.

Spelling Spotlight

Circle the word **come** where it is spelled correctly.

come   kome

cool

came

come

rome

cone

come

coom   comb

long

Practice writing the word **long**.

long

Write the word to complete the sentence.

My hair is too __ __ __ __ !

Now write your own sentence using the word **long**.

Hidden Words

Find the words that have **long** hidden inside.

Circle the whole word, then underline the letters **l-o-n-g**.

lonely

aloud

along

belong

alone

Review: Match Up

Find the word that belongs in each sentence and write it on the line.
Draw a line to connect each pencil with the correct eraser.

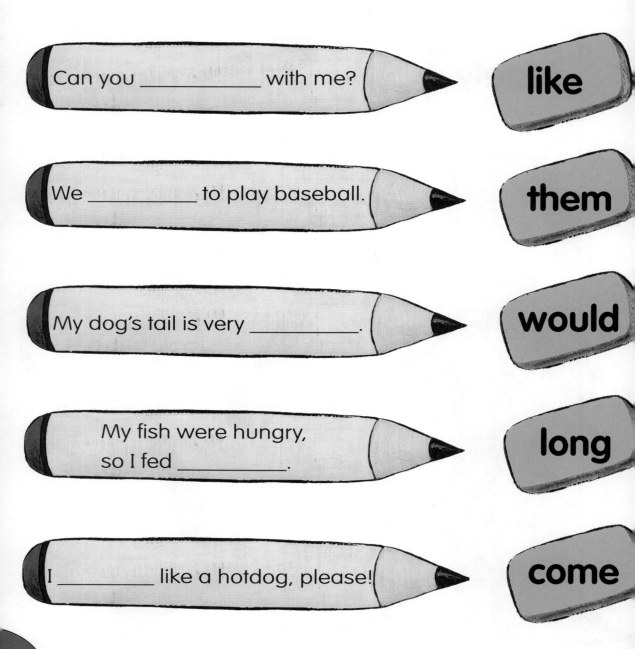

Can you _____ with me?

like

We _____ to play baseball.

them

My dog's tail is very _____.

would

My fish were hungry,
so I fed _____.

long

I _____ like a hotdog, please!

come

Review: Story Code

Read the story and look for the words from the word box.

Follow the code each time you see one of the words.

 them circle it   <u>like</u> underline it   would✓ put a check   come make a box   long wavy line

It was a long, hot day.

"I would like to go to the beach," I said.

"I would too," said Mom.

"Can my friends come with us?" I asked.

"Sure! That sounds like fun," Mom said.

"I'll call them right now," I said.

"It's a long way to the beach," said Mom.

"Tell them we would like to go soon!"

will

Practice writing the word **will**.

will -

Write the word to complete the sentence.

I ___ ___ ___ ___ **dance tonight.**

Now write your own sentence using the word **will**.

Tic Tac Toe

Circle the row that has the word **will** three times.

Then write **will** three times on the lines below.

will	wilt	will
well	will	wil
will	will	wiil

very

Practice writing the word **very**.

very very very very

Write the word to complete the sentence.

My cat is v e r y fat!

Now write your own sentence using the word **very**.

Marcus is very cool!

Word Search

Find the word **very** three times in the word search.

Then write **very** three times on the lines below.

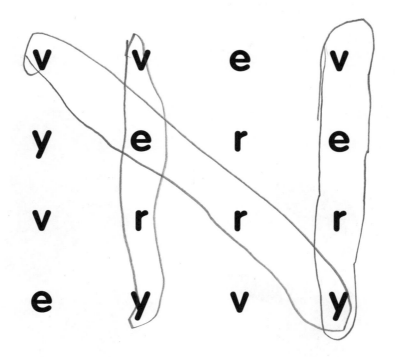

very

very

very

your

Practice writing the word **your**.

your

Write the word to complete the sentence.

I like __ __ __ __ hat!

Now write your own sentence using the word **your**.

Maze

Connect the letters to make **your** and solve the maze!

Then write **your** three times on the lines below.

t   n

o   y

v

e   w

o

u   a

p   m

r   g

Finish!

from

Practice writing the word **from**.

from

Write the word to complete the sentence.

I got a letter
___ ___ ___ ___ my pen pal!

Now write your own sentence using the word **from**.

Sporty Spelling

Circle the word **from** where it is spelled correctly.

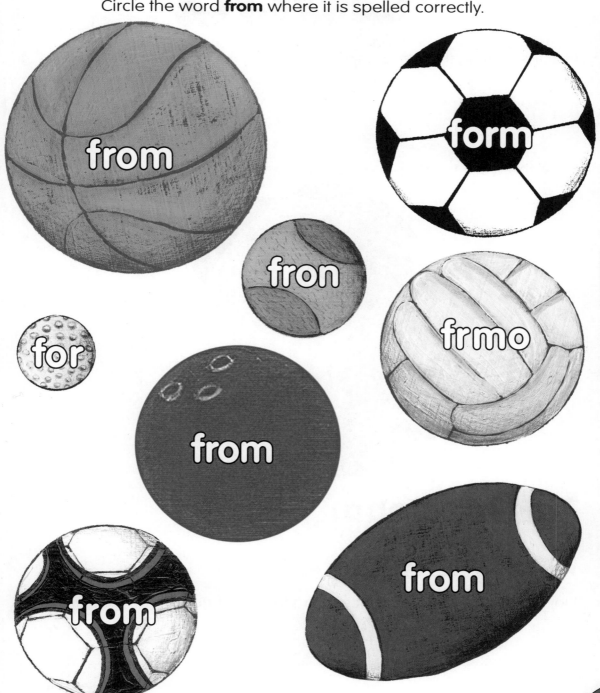

from

form

fron

for

frmo

from

from

from

good

Practice writing the word **good**.

Write the word to complete the sentence.

This ice cream
is very __ __ __ __ !

Now write your own sentence using the word **good**.

Hidden Words

Find the words that have **good** hidden inside.

Circle the whole word, then underline the letters **g-o-o-d**.

goldfish

golden

goodnight

goodbye

goodness

Review: Match Up

Find the word that belongs in each sentence and write it on the line.
Draw a line to connect each pencil with the correct eraser.

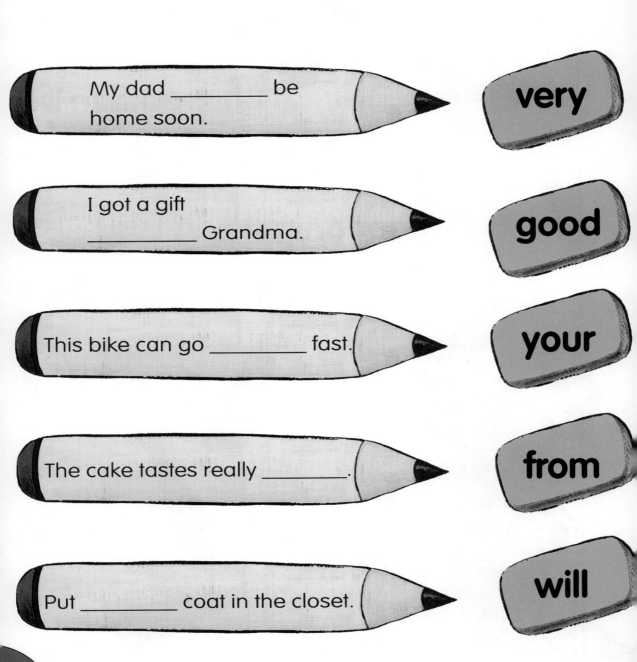

My dad _____ be home soon.

very

I got a gift _____ Grandma.

good

This bike can go _____ fast.

your

The cake tastes really _____.

from

Put _____ coat in the closet.

will

Review: Story Code

Read the story and look for the words from the word box.

Follow the code each time you see one of the words.

will	very	your ✓	good	from
circle it	underline it	put a check	make a box	wavy line

Jeff was having a very good birthday.

His friends from school were at his party.

"Will you open your gifts now?" asked his mom.

"Yes, I will," said Jeff.

"Is that one from your brother?" asked his Mom.

"No," said Jeff. "It's from my good friend Sam."

"It's a baseball hat from your favorite team!" said Sam.

"What a good idea," said Jeff's mom.

"I will wear it every day," said Jeff.

take

Practice writing the word **take**.

take

Write the word to complete the sentence.

I __ __ __ __ my books
to school in my backpack.

Now write your own sentence using the word **take**.

Tic Tac Toe

Circle the row that has the word **take** three times.
Then write **take** three times on the lines below.

tack	take	take
take	take	talk
tack	take	take

29

how

Practice writing the word **how**.

how

Write the word to complete the sentence.

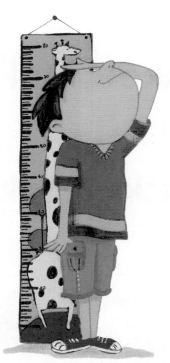

Tell me __ __ __ tall I am.

Now write your own sentence using the word **how**.

Word Search

Find the word **how** three times in the word search.

Then write **how** three times on the lines below.

o   w   h   o

h   h   o   w

o   o   h   w

w   o   w   h

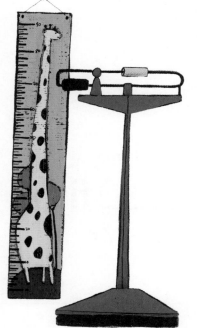

about

Practice writing the word **about**.

about

Write the word to complete the sentence.

This book is __ __ __ __ __ fish.

Now write your own sentence using the word **about**.

Maze

Connect the letters to make **about** and solve the maze!

Then write **about** three times on the lines below.

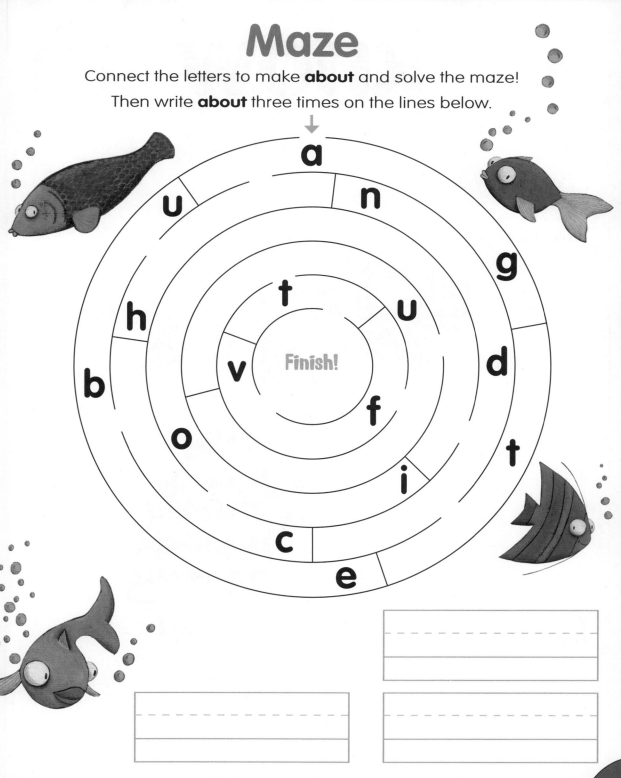

know

Practice writing the word **know**.

know

Write the word to complete the sentence.

I __ __ __ __ the answer!

Now write your own sentence using the word **know**.

Springtime Spelling

Circle the word **know** where it is spelled correctly.

any

Practice writing the word **any**.

any

Write the word to complete the sentence.

I don't have __ __ __ cookies!

Now write your own sentence using the word **any**.

Hidden Words

Find the words that have **any** hidden inside.

Circle the whole word, then underline the letters **a-n-y**.

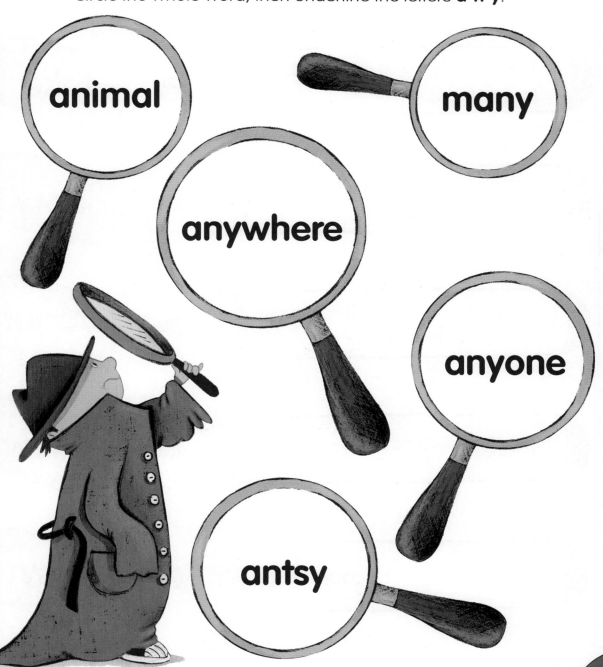

animal

many

anywhere

anyone

antsy

Review: Match Up

Find the word that belongs in each sentence and write it on the line.
Draw a line to connect each pencil with the correct eraser.

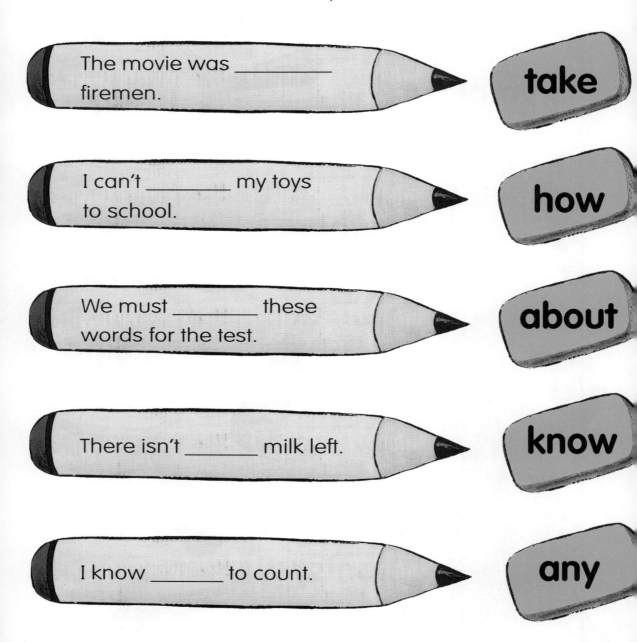

The movie was _____ firemen.

take

I can't _____ my toys to school.

how

We must _____ these words for the test.

about

There isn't _____ milk left.

know

I know _____ to count.

any

Review: Story Code

Read the story and look for the words from the word box.
Follow the code each time you see one of the words.

 take — circle it | how — underline it | about ✓ — put a check | know — make a box | any — wavy line

Dad and I wanted to take our dog to the park.

We didn't know how to get there.

"How can we get to the park?" Dad asked a man.

"I don't know about any parks near here,"
the man said.

"Is there any place our dog can play and run?"
I asked.

"How about the beach?" he asked.

"Great! We'll take our dog there," said Dad.

their

Practice writing the word **their**.

their

Write the word to complete the sentence.

The twins have many people in __ __ __ __ __ family.

Now write your own sentence using the word **their**.

Tic Tac Toe

Circle the row that has the word **their** three times.
Then write **their** three times on the lines below.

their	their	there
thier	their	thire
theri	then	their

here

Practice writing the word **here**.

here

Write the word to complete the sentence.

I keep my pencils in __ __ __ __.

Now write your own sentence using the word **here**.

Word Search

Find the word **here** three times in the word search.

Then write **here** three times on the lines below.

h   r   e   h

r   e   e   e

h   r   r   r

e   o   h   e

after

Practice writing the word **after**.

after

Write the word to complete the sentence.

We can have cake
___ ___ ___ ___ ___ dinner.

Now write your own sentence using the word **after**.

Maze

Connect the letters to make **after** and solve the maze!
Then write **after** three times on the lines below.

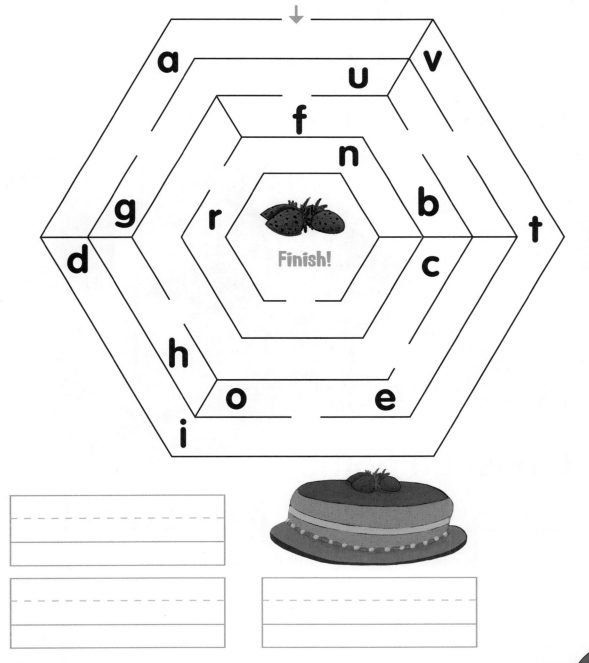

before

Practice writing the word **before**.

before

Write the word to complete the sentence.

I must go home

___ ___ ___ ___ ___ ___ **it gets dark!**

Now write your own sentence using the word **before**.

Spelling Splash

Circle the word **before** where it is spelled correctly.

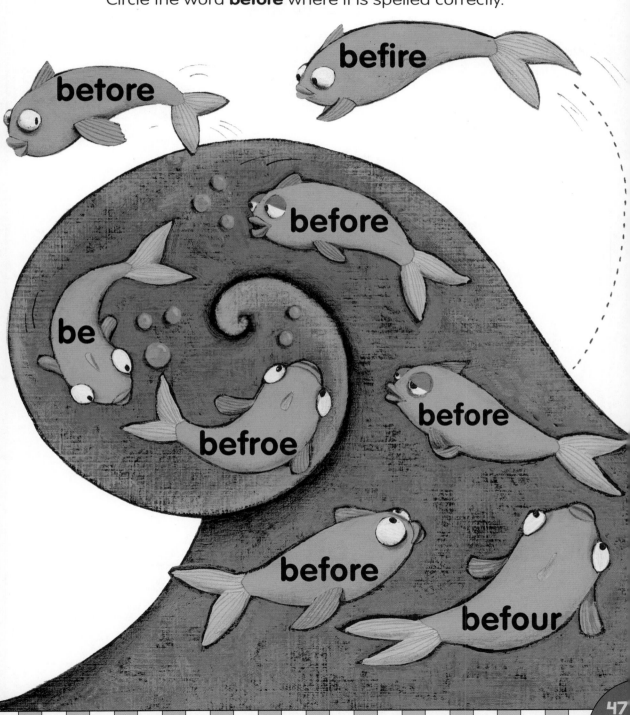

old

Practice writing the word **old**.

old

Write the word to complete the sentence.

Today, I am eight years __ __ __!

Now write your own sentence using the word **old**.

Hidden Words

Find the words that have **old** hidden inside.

Circle the whole word, then underline the letters **o-l-d**.

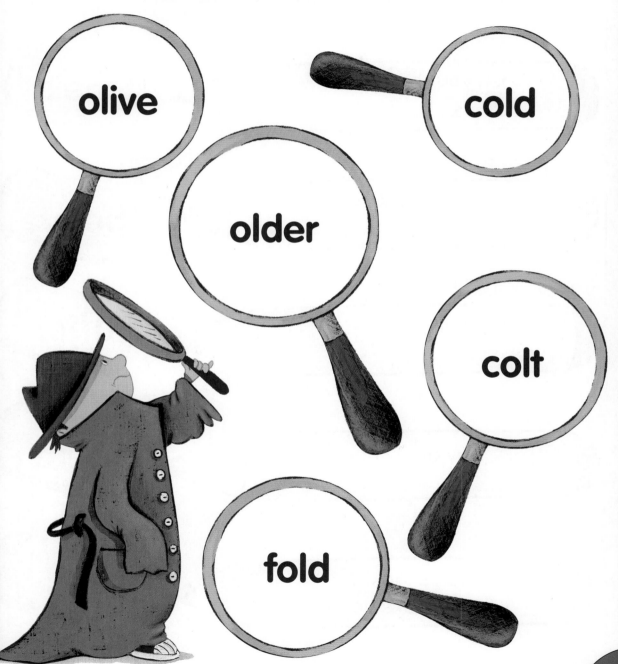

olive

cold

older

colt

fold

Review: Match Up

Find the word that belongs in each sentence and write it on the line.
Draw a line to connect each pencil with the correct eraser.

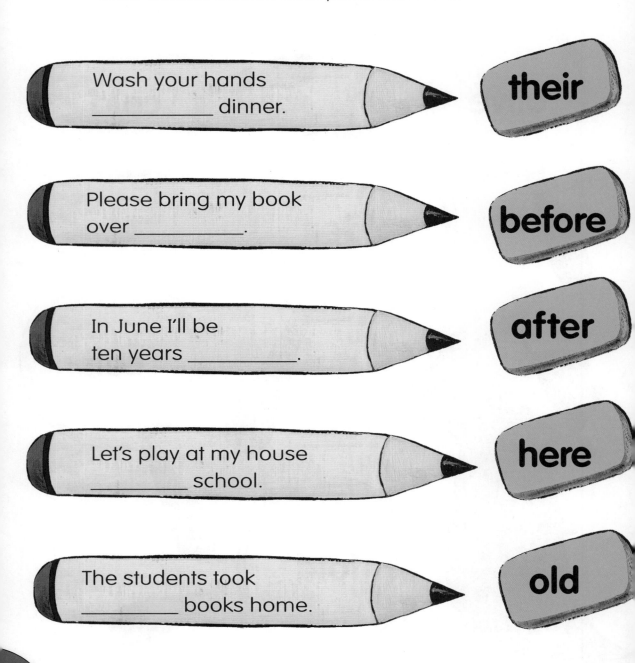

Wash your hands _____ dinner.

their

Please bring my book over _____.

before

In June I'll be ten years _____.

after

Let's play at my house _____ school.

here

The students took _____ books home.

old

Review: Story Code

Read the story and look for the words from the word box.

Follow the code each time you see one of the words.

(their) circle it   **here** underline it   **after✓** put a check   **before** make a box   **old** wavy line

On their way to school, Rob and Ben saw a very old house.

"I haven't seen this house here before," said Ben.

"Let's come back here after school," said Rob.

"I don't want to come back here ever!" said Ben.

"You're too old to be scared," said Rob.

Before Ben could say anything, they heard a loud noise inside the old house.

After the noise stopped, they picked up their books and ran to school.

been

Practice writing the word **been**.

been

Write the word to complete the sentence.

I've __ __ __ __ playing in the rain

Now write your own sentence using the word **been**.

Tic Tac Toe

Circle the row that has the word **been** three times.
Then write **been** three times on the lines below.

been	bene	bean
beep	beem	been
been	been	been

who

Practice writing the word **who**.

who

Write the word to complete the sentence.

I always look
to see ___ ___ ___ is at the door.

Now write your own sentence using the word **who**.

Word Search

Find the word **who** three times in the word search.

Then write **who** three times on the lines below.

h	w	o	h
w	o	h	e
h	o	h	o
o	w	h	o

again

Practice writing the word **again**.

again

Write the word to complete the sentence.

Try to hit the ball __ __ __ __ __ .

Now write your own sentence using the word **again**.

Maze

Connect the letters to make **again** and solve the maze!

Then write **again** three times on the lines below.

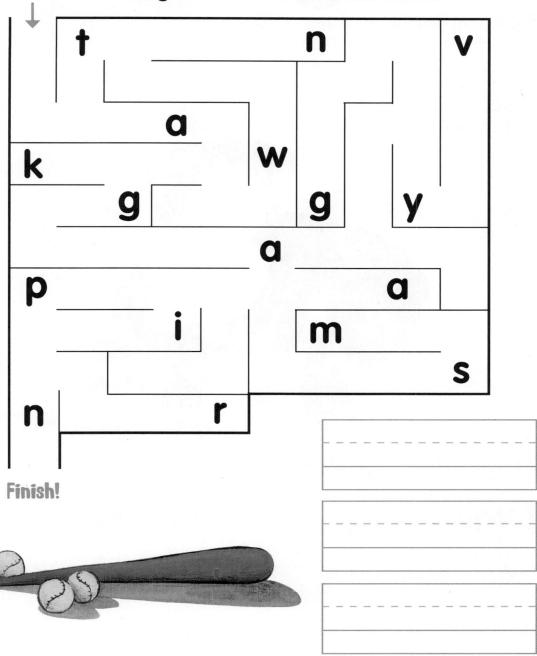

Finish!

give

Practice writing the word **give**.

give

Write the word to complete the sentence.

I will ___ ___ ___ ___ you a kiss.

Now write your own sentence using the word **give**.

Spelling Sprinkles

Circle the word **give** where it is spelled correctly.

Review: Match Up

Find the word that belongs in each sentence and write it on the line.
Draw a line to connect each pencil with the correct eraser.

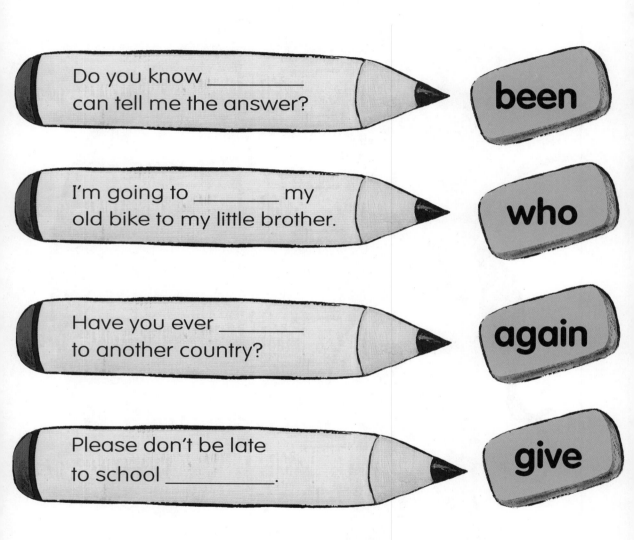

Do you know _____ can tell me the answer?

been

I'm going to _____ my old bike to my little brother.

who

Have you ever _____ to another country?

again

Please don't be late to school _____.

give

Review: Story Code

Read the story and look for the words from the word box.
Follow the code each time you see one of the words.

(been) circle it   who underline it   again✓ put a check   [give] make a box

"Who has been messing up the kitchen again?"
asked Mom.

"Not me! I've been in my room," I said.

"I think I know who it was," said my brother.

"Give us a hint," I said.

"He's only been here for two weeks," said my brother.
"Guess who?"

"Oh, no! The puppy has been making a mess again!"
I said.

"Let's give him a bath," said my brother.

The puppy didn't want a bath. He ran and ran.

"Here we go again!" I said.

Answer Key

Page 5

them	the	them
thee	them	hem
thm	them	them

Page 7

l	k	l	e
i	i	i	l
k	e	k	i
e	i	e	e

Page 9

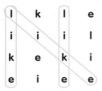

Page 11

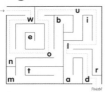

Spelling Spotlight

come · kome · cool · came · come · rome · cone · come · coom · comb

Page 13

lonely · aloud · along · belong · alone

Page 14

Can you **come** with me? — like
We **like** to play baseball. — them
My dog's tail is very **long**. — would
My fish were hungry, so I fed **them**. — long
would like a hotdog, please! — come

Page 15

It was a long, hot day.

"I would like to go to the beach," I said.

"I would, too," said Mom.

"Can my friends come with us?" I asked.

"Sure! That sounds like fun," Mom said.

"I'll call them right now" I said.

"It's a long way to the beach," said Mom. "Tell them we would like to go soon!"

Page 17

will	wilt	will
well	will	wil
will	will	wiil

Page 19

v	v	e	v
y	e	r	e
v	r	r	r
e	y	v	y

Page 21

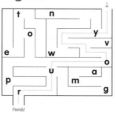

Page 23

Sporty Spelling

from · form · from · fron · trmo · toi · from · from · from

Page 25

goldfish · golden · goodnight · goodbye · goodness

Page 26

My dad **will** be home soon. — very
I got a gift **from** Grandma. — good
This bike can go **very** fast. — your
The cake tastes really **good**. — from
Put **your** coat in the closet. — will

Page 27

Jeff was having a very good birthday.

His friends from school were at his party.

"Will you open your gifts now?" asked his mom.

"Yes, I will," said Jeff.

"Is that one from your brother?" asked his Mom.

"No," said Jeff. "It's from my good friend Sam."

"It's a baseball hat from your favorite team!" said Sam.

"What a good idea," said Jeff's mom.

"I will wear it every day," said Jeff.

Page 29

tack	take	take
take	take	talk
tack	take	take

Page 31

o	w	h	o
h	h	o	w
o	o	h	w
w	o	w	h

Page 33

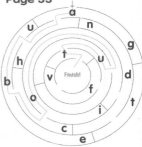

Page 35

Springtime Spelling

now · know · knwo · know · know · knaw · kow · know

62

Page 37

animal — many — anywhere — anyone — antsy

Page 38

The movie was __about__ firemen. — take

I can't __take__ my toys to school. — how

We must __known__ these words for the test. — about

There isn't __any__ milk left. — know

I know __how__ to count. — any

Page 39

Dad and I wanted to (take) our dog to the park.

We didn't [know how] to get there.

"How can we get to the park?" Dad asked a man.

"I don't [know] about any parks near here," the man said.

"Is there any place our dog can play and run?" I asked.

"How about the beach?" he asked.

"Great! We'll (take) our dog there!"

Page 41

their	their	there
their	their	thire
theri	then	their

Page 43

h	r	e	h
r	e	e	e
h	r	r	r
e	o	h	e

Page 45

Page 47

Spelling Splash

Page 49

olive — cold — older — colt — fold

Page 50

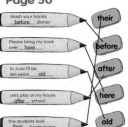

Wash your hands __before__ dinner. — their

Please bring my book over __here__. — before

In June I'll be ten years __old__. — after

Let's play at my house __after__ school. — here

The students took __their__ books home. — old

Page 51

On (their) way to school, Rob and Ben saw a very __old__ house.

"I haven't seen this house here [before]," said Ben.

"Let's come back here after school," said Rob.

"I don't want to come back here ever!" said Ben.

"You're too old to be scared," said Rob.

[Before] Ben could say anything, they heard a loud noise inside the old house.

After the noise stopped, they picked up (their) books and ran to school.

Page 53

been	bene	bean
beep	beem	been
been	been	been

Page 55

h	w	o	h
w	o	h	e
h	o	h	o
o	w	h	o

Page 57

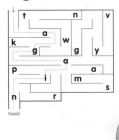

Page 59

Spelling Sprinkles

give — gave — gife — gift — give — give — glev — give

Page 60

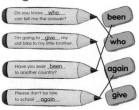

Do you know __who__ can tell me the answer? — been

I'm going to __give__ my old bike to my little brother. — who

Have you ever __been__ to another country? — again

Please don't be late to school __again__. — give

Page 61

"Who has (been) messing up the kitchen again?" asked Mom.

"Not me! I've (been) in my room," I said.

"I think I know who it was," said my brother.

"Give us a hint," I said.

"He's only (been) here for two weeks," said my brother. "Guess who?"

"Oh, no! The puppy has (been) making a mess again!" I said.

"Let's [give] him a bath," said my brother.

The puppy didn't want a bath. He ran and ran.

"Here we go again!" I said.

_____,

(Name)

now you know 24 new sight words!

Give yourself an A+!

Great job!